Enough!

How We Can Turn

Outrage Into Action

Enough!

How We Can Turn Outrage Into Action

S. E. McClellan

Rad Mod Press

Sacramento, CA | Sedona, AZ | Charlottesville, VA

© 2025 S. E. McClellan

Published by Rad Mod Press

Sacramento, CA | Sedona, AZ | Charlottesville, VA

All rights reserved. No part of this book may be reproduced, distributed, or transmitted in any form or by any means, including photocopying, recording, or other electronic or mechanical methods, without the prior written permission of the publisher, except in the case of brief quotations embodied in critical reviews and certain other noncommercial uses permitted by copyright law.

ISBN (Paperback): 9798992875409

ISBN (E-Book): 9798992875423

The publisher and author make no representations or warranties with respect to the accuracy or completeness of the contents of this book except that information was gathered with diligence and good intent. Any references to websites, organizations, or resources are provided for informational purposes only and do not constitute an endorsement except where explicitly indicated.

First Edition

Printed in the United States of America

Contents

Introduction and Acknowledgements — ix

How Did We Get Here? — 1

Section One: Human Dignity — 8
    Practice 1: Stay Curious & Build Bridges — 10
    Practice 2: Model and Insist on Civility — 15
    Practice 3: Connect with Local Suffering and Possibility — 21

Section Two: Purpose — 29
    Practice 4: Choose Action Over Cynicism — 31
    Practice 5: Let Your 'Why' Drive Your Actions — 37
    Practice 6: Consume Mindfully — 42

Section Three: Joy — 51
    Practice 7: Move Your Body — 53
    Practice 8: Gather — 58
    Practice 9: Take the Risks that Matter — 64

Onwards! — 71

About the Author — 72

Introduction and Acknowledgements

Although I have done much of the writing for this book on my own, many of the ideas were developed or refined through dozens of conversations with friends, colleagues, and even a few casual acquaintances over the past several years. These individuals care deeply about our nation, about human dignity, and about our collective capacity to shape a better future together. I will use 'we' rather than 'I' throughout this book to honor the time and expertise of countless caring and creative people I am lucky to know–including family members, friends, mentors, students, former students, educators, and others. I am grateful to the work of many dedicated community organizers who believe in the power of people to move the world–to skilled facilitators like Kai Degner of Central Virginia and Dr. Ken Futernick of northern California and to cultural creatives like Josh Schacter of Tucson, Arizona.

I want to offer special gratitude to my husband Bryon Gustafson who helped me maintain faith in this effort and take the final steps to see it through to publication. I also want to thank my long-time friend and colleague Iish Ryaru who generously edited multiple drafts and offered his abundant optimism and kindness to envision more constructive actions for us all.

How Did We Get Here?

Regardless of your political leaning or your social or religious affiliations, we suspect you're feeling like something isn't right in our country. You may be drowning in a sea of opinions about what's wrong or who's to blame. Maybe you can't stop checking the news, or you can't get loved ones to unplug from their devices. You might worry about how climate change will impact future generations—or worry that climate change is a distraction when drug overdoses, homelessness, and unemployment are just outside your front door. If you're like many Americans, you talk with people online more than you talk with your neighbors. You're not so sure artificial intelligence and self-driving cars will make life better, but you're pretty sure no one's slowing down to ask your opinion. You might vote and donate time or money to worthy causes, but it doesn't feel like enough.

Scholars and investigative journalists have written about our increasingly overloaded and anxious society in many compelling books and articles. We won't revisit this work in any detail. Instead, we'll summarize a few factors shaping our current moment and share sources you can review in more detail should you choose to do so.

- **Digital Overload & Social Media Fatigue:** A growing body of research shows that significant social media use decreases our face-to-face interactions, increases political polarization, heightens stress levels, and contributes to isolation and loss of in-person community. Algorithm-driven content now fueled by Artificial Intelligence (AI) amplifies negativity and conflict quite effectively since our brains have evolved to focus on and remember negative information more strongly than positive information.[12]

- **Economic Strain & Job Insecurity:** Rising housing costs, wage stagnation, inflation, and job insecurity have left many of us feeling financially anxious. This has happened over a period of decades—since 1980—and under leaders of both major political parties. The wealthiest have experienced significant gains in recent years while middle- and lower-income families have fallen further behind. Whatever the causes (and there are likely several), economic stress often leads to social withdrawal and prioritization of individual survival over collective well-being. Long work hours and gig economy pressures also leave many of us too busy or exhausted to engage in social or civic activities.[3]

- **Erosion of Trust in Institutions:** Studies show a major decline in trust in government, media, technology companies, and other institutions over a period of many years. This lack of institutional trust increases cynicism and reduces civic participation since we tend to disengage when we don't feel like our voices matter or that leaders and systems will respond to our concerns.[4]

---

[1] Haidt, J. (2024). *The anxious generation: How the great rewiring of childhood is causing an epidemic of mental illness.* Random House.

[2] Hari, J. (2023). *Stolen focus: Why you can't pay attention—and how to think deeply again.* Crown.

[3] Horowitz, J. M., Igielnik, R., & Kochhar, R. (2020). *Trends in income and wealth inequality.* Pew Research Center.

[4] Bhutto, F. (2024). Trust in Public Institutions: Causes of Decline and Ways to Restore It. *Research Consortium Archive, 2*(3), 123-131.

- **Political Polarization & Information Overload:** Increasing ideological divides have been fueled by partisan media, the rise of infotainment news on both the left and the right, and online echo chambers. AI algorithms now make it possible for us to live in completely different information universes, digesting notably different news stories and perspectives. Social media platforms are designed to incentivize strong opinions and fuel disagreements through their 'share' and 'like' features and their lack of screening to exclude bots and foreign actors. Some of us find ourselves sucked into endless debates and outrage. Others among us retreat from online discourse out of exhaustion, fear, or frustration with entrenched divides.[5]

- **Over-Emphasis on Consumption:** A culture that prioritizes consumption—particularly through debt-driven spending—leaves many of us financially overextended. Fast-paced over-consumption also has us eating unhealthier foods and throwing more cheap products into our landfills. Many of us get caught up in cycles of consuming and working longer hours and dedicating less time to our social and civic lives. Over-consumption in the digital world often leaves us feeling 'informed' but without the time or energy to take action in the real-world. Studies also show that, beyond meeting basic needs, material and online consumption do not actually lead to increased happiness. In fact, over-consumption can increase social comparison and dissatisfaction.

---

[5] Rich, M. D. (2018). *Truth decay: An initial exploration of the diminishing role of facts and analysis in American public life.* Rand Corporation.

- **Mental Health Crises & Social Isolation:** Rising rates of anxiety, depression, and burnout appear to be heightened or caused by excessive time on social media, loss of social supports, a decline in meaningful engagement at work, and fears about the future fueled by a crisis-driven news cycle. A lack of physical activity and unhealthy diets also contribute to poor mental health across the U.S. A decline of local community spaces—sometimes called *third places*—like libraries, parks, community centers, and other local gathering spots also reduces our informal opportunities for social connection. Without these physical places, we struggle to form and maintain place-based bonds and interact with each other across differences.[6]

Political leaders and influencers across the political spectrum are more than willing to take advantage of our isolation, anxiety, and uncertainty. They are fueling polarization with divisive language and leaning into culture wars. Few political leaders are speaking directly about the sources of our discontent outlined above. President Trump's campaign centered on a long list of grievances and he has committed to making "America Great Again." Regardless of how you feel about President Trump's campaign promises or policies, we invite you to consider if and how he is addressing the above problems. We also invite you to keep an eye on how any President's actions support or contradict key principles of our Constitutional Republic and representative democracy.

- The three separate but equal branches of government established by the U.S. Constitution designed to ensure no single

---

[6] Putnam, R. D. (2000). *Bowling alone: The collapse and revival of American community*. Simon Schuster.

branch of government becomes too powerful: the legislative branch makes the law, the executive branch enforces the law, and the judicial branch interprets the law.

- Citizens' ability to participate in free, fair, and frequent elections.
- Independent sources of political information (the press) that are not controlled or unduly influenced by the government or by any single group or leader.
- Citizens' right to express themselves publicly on a broad range of politically relevant subjects and to form and participate in independent political organizations or interest groups without fear of punishment.

If our nation's civic ideals are to prevail, we–the majority of citizens–will be tasked with assessing threats to the above principles and acting responsibly. We will also need to hold our republic together so our political actions do not destroy the bonds of human dignity that allow us to live peaceably together despite our differences.

Although many of our social problems are driven by systemic economic and political forces, we do not believe change is beyond our reach if ENOUGH individuals find ways to act together. History offers us some examples. Although it's easy to look at social movements like the U.S. Labor Movement, U.S. Civil Rights Movement, or the Fall of Apartheid in South Africa and focus on a small number of charismatic leaders, these movements changed society through the efforts of millions of individuals. Change involved grassroots organizing, public education, strikes, legal action, financial boycotts, and conversations—big and small.

We believe the time is right for a movement that aims to reclaim what is ENOUGH—human dignity, purpose, and joy—one person and one community at a time. At its heart, this work is about human connection and responsibility. Being a responsible citizen in a representative democracy requires us to do more than vote or donate money. It calls on us to learn about our fellow citizens, understand our basic system of government, give back to our communities, and take action when our political leaders pull us away from our civic values. Supporting human dignity also means refusing to view people as *others*, (re)learning to disagree better without breaking our closest bonds and finding ways to eliminate or tame the forces that pull us apart.

Our most audacious goal is to create a new form of collective action that demands more from us and more from our leaders across the political spectrum as well as from the CEOs who have increasing power to shape our lives.

Even if the road is long, we aim to offer you concrete strategies and tools you can apply immediately to feel just a little more connected, empowered, and joyful during difficult times. Some of these steps are grounded in a great deal of evidence and some represent our own ideas based on our experiences as educators, practitioners, and civic participants. All of these steps add up to generate impact when thousands, hundreds of thousands, or even millions of us commit to experimenting with new practices and new forms of engagement in our daily lives.

We hope you will grab what resonates, experiment some with the rest, and—most importantly—invite others in your neighborhood, book club, faith group, workplace, or social movement to join you!

Below is an outline of the sections and practices in this guide. At the end of each section, we invite you to use a simple Action Planning template to identify practices you'll take for a test drive as you prioritize action over outrage.

Section One: Human Dignity

Practice 1: Stay Curious and Build Bridges

Practice 2: Model and Insist on Civility

Practice 3: Connect with *Local* Suffering and Possibility

Section Two: Purpose

Practice 4: Choose Action Over Cynicism

Practice 5: Let Your *Why* Drive Your Actions

Practice 6: Consume Mindfully

Section Three: Joy

Practice 7: Move Your Body

Practice 8: Gather

Practice 9: Take the Risks That Matter

Section One: Human Dignity

Respect for human dignity has been a powerful unifying force at pivotal moments throughout history.[7] This principle is not just an abstract ideal; it has guided movements for justice, democracy, and human rights around the world. Human dignity is not simply about fairness, but about recognizing the full worth of *every* person in a society—especially those who have less access to society's resources such as healthy food, safe neighborhoods, good schools, or stable employment. This principle presses us to ensure our institutions are not merely efficient, but fundamentally humane. Respect for human dignity is not just a moral value; it is a practical necessity for building fair, inclusive, and stable societies. It is also rooted in spiritual commitments for many of us, and human dignity offers us common ground in our religiously and culturally diverse nation.

Research shows that humans do not simply crave material security or power; we seek recognition of our intrinsic worth and a sense that we are seen and understood. Where we fail to honor human dignity—by excluding, oppressing, shaming, or dehumanizing individuals in any effort—we might expect to face unrest and resistance.[8] The pursuit of dignity, therefore, is a force

---

[7] Newland, C. A. (2012). Values and virtues in public administration: Post-NPM global fracture and search for human dignity and reasonableness. *Public Administration Review, 72*(2), 293-302.

[8] Fukuyama, F. (2018). *Identity: The demand for dignity and the politics of resentment.* Farrar, Straus and Giroux.

we can use to unite struggles for a healthier and more just society.[9] Where, for example, different groups lack access to healthy food, clean water, or quality education they will influence public sentiment and public policy more powerfully when they coordinate to advance their shared interests, despite their differences. We can be unrelenting in our pursuit of human dignity, but expansive in our vision to unite and uplift all people.

A commitment to human dignity requires us to adopt a *big tent* approach—one that welcomes and includes people of all races, classes, and backgrounds in the effort to build a more just and humane society. Too often, political and social movements become fragmented or exclusive, limiting their reach and impact. Powerful interests often benefit from fragmentation and infighting that leaves us unable to mobilize together. But dignity is universal; it is not confined to any one group's struggle. When we recognize that the fights for economic fairness, racial justice, and human rights are interconnected, we create space for more people to see themselves in the work and join in constructing solutions. Reaffirming our commitment to human dignity offers a shared ethical foundation— one that may help us move beyond partisan battles to work on solving public problems together. Below are some concrete practices we can take to support human dignity in our daily lives.

---

[9] King Jr, M. L. (1967/2010). *Where do we go from here: Chaos or community?*. Beacon Press.

Practice 1: Stay Curious & Build Bridges

"Let go of certainty. The opposite isn't uncertainty. It's openness, curiosity and a willingness to embrace paradox..."

– Tony Schwartz

Why it matters:

We believe curiosity is one of the most important tools we have for building a fair and humane world. When we take the time to ask each other questions and listen deeply to each other's experiences—beyond what is possible in most online platforms—we begin to see and understand each other in a different way. We agree with David Brooks that really knowing someone means being curious about their life, not just judging them based on quick impressions and surface-level identities.[10] Seeing someone deeply is one way of honoring human dignity. Monica Guzmán also describes how connecting with people who think differently than we do might even help us discover common ground or create unexpected solutions together.[11]

Curiosity has played a major role in shaping human societies by driving discoveries and inspiring works of art, music, and literature. Throughout history, there have been times when leaders or societies tried to limit curiosity by banning books, restricting

---

[10] Brooks, D. (2023). *How to know a person: The art of seeing others deeply and being deeply seen*. Random House.

[11] Guzmán, M. (2022). *I never thought of it that way: How to have fearlessly curious conversations in dangerously divided times*. BenBella Books.

education, or punishing new ideas. For example, during the Middle Ages, the Catholic Church tried to suppress scientific discoveries that challenged its teachings. China lost a generation of scholars and artists during their Cultural Revolution when curiosity and independent thinking were severely restricted. When curiosity is stamped out, progress slows and people stop asking important questions and exploring new solutions. Reclaiming our curiosity means asking more questions, searching for overlapping interests, and identifying unlikely allies.

What it looks like in action:

If Black and white Freedom Riders and others fighting for social justice in the 1960s had not taken the time to talk curiously with people who held different opinions, it's unlikely we would have seen the shifts in public opinion that contributed to ending segregation. We also see where curiosity can break down intellectual barriers when we look at the friendship between Ruth Bader Ginsburg and Antonin Scalia, two U.S. Supreme Court Justices who often disagreed on major legal matters. Despite their differences they asked each other tough questions and listened with curiosity.

According to curiosity expert Scott Shigeoka, we often trigger a positive spiral of interactions when we begin asking people curious heartfelt questions about their daily lives.[12] People who feel seen and valued are more likely to engage others in curious

---

[12] Futernick, K. (Host). (2025). *The transformative power of curiosity: A conversation with Scott Shigeoka* [Audio podcast]. Courageous Conversations About Our Schools.

conversations. And, although kids are incredibly curious, Scott says it's "a myth that we're only curious when we're young."

Starting with curiosity does not mean we need to put ourselves in a threatening position or tolerate abusive behavior. It does, however, challenge us to engage in curious practices, test our assumptions, and stop avoiding people who think differently. We might notice when we make quick, superficial judgements about another person's experiences or perspectives on a public problem. We might ask more curious, open-ended questions. Groups like Braver Angels model ways of practicing dialogue grounded in curiosity to reduce political polarization.[13] Curiosity also means actively moving beyond your usual sources of information and nudging others to do the same.

Actions you can take:

On Your Own:

- Get a free account with Ground News to read news from multiple perspectives and examine your own sources with a more curious and critical eye.[14]

- Attend a public meeting specifically to listen to concerns from an unfamiliar group or community.

- Watch people who are deeply curious about others, taking note of the curious questions they ask.

---

[13] https://braverangels.org
[14] https://ground.news/

- When you next vote for a political candidate (including when you vote among members of your own party), ask: *is this person curious?*
- Jot down some curious questions you'll plan to ask people at an upcoming gathering or event:
  ◊ *What drew you to this role/community/work?*
  ◊ *How did you come to value X?*
  ◊ *What brings you joy?*

<u>With Others:</u>

- Ask someone who holds a position that troubles or surprises you <u>not</u> *why* they came to hold a particular perspective but *how* they came to hold that perspective.
- Invite someone who holds very different political views to join you in using <u>Ground News</u> for a month and meet to discuss if/how it changes your perspectives on events.[15]
- If you are actively engaged in a political group or social movement: ask who has not yet joined you with an eye to unexpected allies. Take the time to meet with these individuals or groups and learn more about what would lead them to engage.
- Stay curious about online resources, applying and sharing <u>guidance on how to spot fake news and AI-generated images and videos</u>.[16]

---

[15] https://ground.news/
[16] https://buildersmovement.org/2025/02/25/5-tips-spot-fake-news-ai-generated-media/

- Join your local Braver Angels Chapter to bridge partisan divides.[17]

- Join the Builders Movement to "choose solutions over sides" and explore new ways of solving public problems.[18]

- Draw on free Citizen Journalism resources to create a group that explores how events and public policy decisions are impacting members of your community–especially if your community has lost its local press.[19]

- Attend town hall meetings with others to ask open-ended questions aimed at examining the consequences of political choices (e.g., *"how should we address crime in our neighborhoods if immigrant families are afraid to report crimes to police?"* or *"what steps will our city need to take to counteract the impacts of reduced funding for X?"*).

- Ask someone with whom you disagree on many things to partner with you in taking action (big or small) on just one social or political topic you do actually agree on.

---

[17] https://braverangels.org
[18] https://buildersmovement.org
[19] https://www.independentmedia.us/education/citizen-journalism-101-training-series

Practice 2: Model and Insist on Civility

"Play fair. Don't hit people. Say you're sorry when you hurt somebody." – Robert Fulghum

"It has become appallingly obvious that our technology has exceeded our humanity." – Albert Einstein

Why it Matters:

Civility means something much different than politeness. Politeness involves surface-level behaviors or social etiquette.[20] Civility, on the other hand, involves a deeper moral sense and engagement in a political society. Definitions of civility vary but, according to Shils, civility points towards the possibility of common good.[21] Civility also means acknowledging the complexity of social values and virtues–understanding that no single virtue or virtuous act stands alone without sometimes contradicting another virtue we or someone else holds dear. This form of civility helps to make reasonable compromise possible in any community. If each of us stakes our every virtue and position with absolute certainty, we risk falling out of community or becoming ungovernable. The ability to understand virtues in tension also helps us see the humanity in people even when we come into conflict over ideas and actions.

---

[20] Hudson, A. (2023). *The soul of civility: Timeless principles to heal society and ourselves.* St. Martin's Press.

[21] Shils, E. (1958). Ideology and civility: On the politics of the intellectual.

Of course, we might struggle to differentiate civility from politeness, especially where politeness might legitimize hostile or unjust behavior. We might also struggle to maintain civility in the face of unrelenting certainty or overt hostility from political leaders and influencers who seek to benefit from social divisions–people sometimes called *conflict entrepreneurs*.[22] Although it may be tempting to relinquish civility in the face of destructive behavior, this typically harms long-term prospects for constructive solutions to public problems. Acting without civility threatens to degrade our own ability to stay centered on our moral commitments and erodes trust in critical institutions. Incivility also undermines our efforts to respect human dignity and create a more just society by sucking us into endless cycles of escalating conflict.

What it looks like in action:

Being civil does not require us to hold our tongue or be polite in the face of injustice. In fact, being too polite can keep us from having the difficult conversations that may prove crucial to a healthy democracy. Civility calls on us to voice disagreement—sometimes strongly—without losing sight of someone else's basic humanity. Many authors describe being civil as a willingness to challenge ideas or behaviors without attacking people. Civility can involve communicating hard truths and calling out injustice boldly, but without cruelty. Powerful social action does not have to be polite, but we believe it can still meet basic definitions of civility.

---

[22] Ripley, A. (2021). *High conflict: Why we get trapped and how we get out.* Simon and Schuster.

Organizations like Braver Angels are also working to help us disagree better.[23] National Braver Angels debates allow people to practice civility by creating a respectful place to thoughtfully disagree. Instead of trying to win an argument, the goal is to better understand different viewpoints. Each debate focuses on a controversial topic and participants share ideas openly, honestly, and respectfully while specially trained Debate Chairs guide the discussion to support good faith, accurate disagreement. Often, people who normally disagree politically find themselves agreeing on some points and disagreeing on others. Braver Schools Communities is also ramping up these efforts to help middle school and high school students learn to disagree with both confidence and civility.[24]

Actions you can take:

On Your Own:

- Take the Dignity Index Pledge and encourage others to use and share Dignity Index resources.[25]

- Tune into the Courageous Conversations About Our Schools podcast to see how Ken Futernick facilitates civic dialogue about controversial K-12 issues.[26]

---

[23] https://braverangels.org
[24] https://braverangels.org/braver-schools/
[25] https://www.dignity.us
[26] https://www.schoolconversations.org

- Observe or participate in a National Braver Angels Debate to see how explicit communication values and debate rules can support civility.[27]

With Others Online:

- When you disagree with someone's perspective, use direct and respectful language focused on the argument rather than the person.
- If someone you know shares information you believe is inaccurate that might harm or misinform other participants, respond with a genuinely curious question that pushes towards deeper inquiry.

    Example: *"I haven't seen much data to suggest that X is happening. What other sources or information could help us determine whether this is true?"*

    Or, share links to well-researched information by multiple sources and offer to return for a conversation once participants have reviewed additional information. This frequently generates more curious engagement from participants or simply ends the discussion–either outcome could support increased online civility.

- If you believe someone's argument involves a logical fallacy (e.g., comparing two events with little in common to make a point), you might post information on logical fallacies in a neutral tone, inviting other discussion participants to decide for

---

[27] https://braverangels.org/events/category/debate/national-online-debate/

themselves whether an argument is sound rather than making the call yourself.[28]

- Refuse to interact with online participants who are overtly hostile by modeling civil disengagement: *"I'm here for constructive discussion, not personal attacks. I'm open to a respectful conversation if you want that. Otherwise, I'll step away"* or *"I'm happy to discuss disagreements, but not in a hostile or bad-faith way. Take care."*

- Express gratitude for well-formulated arguments and fact-checking efforts even when you don't see eye-to-eye with the source (e.g., *"Although I'm upset about the nature of recent deportations, Maria has shared some solid and relevant data on immigration challenges we should consider as we debate solutions. Thank you, Maria!"*)

With Others In-person:

- Check your understanding of someone's perspective in a face-to-face conversation by resharing the perspective or feelings you believe you heard along with a question: *"Am I getting that right?"* or *"Is there something I may not be understanding?"*

- Urge your organization or political campaign to take the Dignity Index pledge and apply Dignity Index practices in your work.[29]

- Confront incivility directly where you encounter it–describe the damage you see it causing and call for constructive rather than divisive communication.

---

[28] https://www.logicalfallacies.org/
[29] https://www.dignity.us

- If you experience hostility in a conversation, redirect or disengage respectfully but firmly: *"I want us to have a good conversation, but I don't think we're hearing each other right now"* or *"I value our relationship, so let's take a break before this gets too heated."*

- If you experience hostility, experiment with the power of silence–sometimes a lengthy pause and unwavering stare will help you breathe deeply, regain your center and communicate boundaries: *"I'm going to finish my point, and then I'm glad to hear your response"* or *"I'm glad to discuss the issue, but I won't engage in personal insults."*

- Call attention to the perverse incentives that lead many conflict entrepreneurs (those who benefit from social outrage) to fuel hostility: *"I realize infotainment hosts/influencers often increase their viewership by getting people stirred up and angry, but that doesn't actually help us solve problems here in our community/organization."*[30]

---

[30] Ripley, A. (2021). *High conflict: Why we get trapped and how we get out.* Simon and Schuster.

Practice 3: Connect with *Local* Suffering and Possibility

"I think the answer is more local stuff. If you participate in a local organization and you participate in local government, you might develop a sense of political efficacy—a sense that you can understand your community and government and influence their direction. This stands in contrast to the way society feels right now, which is like me as an individual and then the national government, and we don't feel embedded in any institutions in between."

– Stanford Sociologist Aaron Horvath, 2024

Throughout history, humans have used the power of storytelling to build understanding and shape social change.[31] Researchers like Paul Zak have shown that hearing or reading personal stories with sufficient attention can activate parts of our brain associated with emotions and social understanding.[32] Exposure to stories can release chemicals linked to empathy in our brain and make us more likely to connect our own experiences to the experiences of others. Images can also have an immediate visceral effect on us when they convey raw emotions and realities that words alone may not express.

---

[31] Fisher, W. R. (2017). Narration, reason, and community. In *Writing the Social Text* (pp. 199-217). Routledge.

[32] Zak, P. J. (2014). Why your brain loves good storytelling. *Harvard Business Review, 28*, 1-5.

Unfortunately, conflict entrepreneurs now manipulate images and stories to stoke fear and outrage, potentially hijacking our commitment to human dignity.[33] Increasingly advanced photo manipulation and deep fake technology fuels strong emotions untethered from actual events. Continued exposure to troubling news at a global scale may also lead us to disengage or numb ourselves to handle an onslaught of unpleasant emotions. A dynamic called *Liar's Dividend* also emerges when conflict entrepreneurs benefit from pumping enough misinformation and fake images into society that we stop trusting our own ability to differentiate truth from fiction. As we have more difficulty assessing the truth in what we read or see in the virtual world, we may become less motivated to engage civically to solve public problems. Some of us may become more susceptible to conspiracy theories.

Since misinformation is harder to sustain in local communities, we encourage social activists to involve people directly in understanding and sharing the local impact of public problems and policy decisions. Unlike events viewed only at a national or global scale, local problems often have tangible impact and actionable solutions that individuals can experience and contribute to directly. This access may give us a greater sense of both agency *and* responsibility. When we strengthen real-world connections in our neighborhoods and communities we may also become more resistant to online disinformation and more curious about how we safeguard ourselves from conflict entrepreneurs.

---

[33] Ripley, A. (2021). *High conflict: Why we get trapped and how we get out.* Simon and Schuster.

What it looks like in action:

Josh Schacter of CommunityShare often uses visual storytelling to help communities highlight their social and environmental issues in powerful and engaging ways.[34][35] Youth who work with Josh share deeply personal experiences with environmental injustice, homelessness, or under-resourced schools while they build strong social bonds and invent community solutions. Students take photos and craft stories–designing posters, videos, or other creative work. Their images are sometimes heart-breaking, surprising, or filled with hope. Josh has helped youth share their experiences with others in public spaces such as malls, bus stops, or government buildings to influence adult decision-making. Artists throughout the world have also used large public murals or music to capture human suffering and new possibilities in their communities.

Since supporting human dignity requires us to engage in public life, we need more trusted educators and civic leaders at the local level to help citizens understand our system of government. Not everyone has the background to make connections between decisions at one level of government and impacts in their local community. Groups like More Perfect are building initiatives and resources to help strengthen Civic Learning across the U.S. Local educators can tap into these resources to strengthen civic understanding in their communities.[36]

---

[34] https://ceinternational1892.org/people/josh-schachter/
[35] https://www.communityshare.org/
[36] https://www.joinmoreperfect.us/goals/universal-civic-learning

Faith communities also have the power to reduce human suffering by calling out injustice or offering individuals more resources and support. Many U.S. Civil Rights marches and rallies were faith-driven demonstrations. Religious organizations have taken public stands in support of refugees, organized food and disaster assistance, and offered legal aid. Interfaith groups have organized to counter hate around the world, developing campaigns and holding vigils. As a leader of the Anglican Church, Archbishop Desmond Tutu used his platform to call for economic sanctions, advocate for nonviolent resistance, and speak out against state violence to help end Apartheid in South Africa.

Actions you can take:

On Your Own:

- Use the 5 Calls website to regularly contact your political representatives and tell them how government decisions are impacting you or members of your community. Don't just talk abstractly–be specific in sharing physical, economic, and/or emotional impacts of particular political decisions you have experienced or witnessed.[37]

- Write an op ed to share how political decisions are impacting members of your community.[38]

- Volunteer for and/or donate to political candidates who demonstrate a commitment to addressing human suffering and injustice impacting your community.

---

[37] https://5calls.org
[38] https://www.theopedproject.org/resources

With Others:

- Organize or join a local group to examine how state or national decisions are impacting members of your local community and design and implement local response strategies (review the Central Shenandoah Valley L.O.C.A.L. Summits organizing site for an excellent example).[39]

- Share testimony, examples, and images in public meetings to show legislators and fellow citizens how government decisions are impacting people in your local community.

- Take photos or create art to capture events that harm or enhance human dignity and coordinate with local organizations to display this imagery in publicly visible places.

- Prioritize human dignity and progress over retribution, giving people room to save face (dignity) even if you believe their political choices contribute to their current suffering.

- If you have a background in U.S. government, offer to provide talks and Q&A sessions on public problems and the role of government to groups in your community (e.g., to senior communities, faith groups, neighborhood associations, etc.).

- If you are a member of a faith community, volunteer to address suffering and urge your spiritual leaders to acknowledge human impacts of major events and political decisions in a way that is consistent with your faith. Ask your leaders what they are doing to help reduce human suffering and support human dignity.

---

[39] https://www.localsummits.org/info

- If you are a parent or mentor, talk to young people about civic engagement opportunities.
- Post hard-to-ignore messaging and images about local suffering or promising solutions in public spaces utilizing billboards, signs, public bulletin boards, etc., using QR code stickers to share more evidence or information.
- Make political failure or hypocrisy visible online or in public spaces by mass-posting the public speeches/quotes and decisions of legislators next to images of local impact.
- Organize 'Day of Listening' community visits to shelters, food banks, and crisis centers to collect direct stories.
- If you are an educator, tap into resources from More Perfect to help strengthen civic learning.[40]

---

[40] https://www.joinmoreperfect.us/goals/universal-civic-learning

Section One Action Plan to Support Human Dignity

We recommend starting with just one or two actions from this section as you experiment with building or strengthening your civic habits. Add and document your own action ideas as well!

Actions I'll Take	
1.	
With Whom?	**By When?**
2.	
With Whom?	**By When?**
3.	
With Whom?	**By When?**
4.	
With Whom?	**By When?**

Section One Action Lessons

Consider jotting down lessons learned from any actions you've taken in this section.

1. **What impact I believe I've had with my actions (for myself and for others):**

2. **What, if anything, surprised me:**

3. **What I learned that will help me in the future:**

Section Two: Purpose

Many modern influencers have written and talked about purpose as essential for human happiness and success. Simon Sinek popularized this topic in management circles when he emphasized the idea of "starting with why" and argued that both people and organizations thrive and achieve when they align their work to a deeper reason beyond profit.[41] Numerous organizational experts suggest that being clear on our purpose helps us make better decisions, stay motivated, and contribute more to our organizations and communities.

The search for purpose is not a new idea. Viktor Frankl, a Holocaust survivor and psychologist wrote, in *Man's Search for Meaning*, that finding meaning–even in the very darkest of circumstances–is what keeps us going.[42] He believed that we don't just discover purpose, but that we *create* purpose through our choices, interactions, struggles, and contributions to others. Purpose is not just about personal success. It plays a role in–and is derived from–our communities.[43] Research shows that people who feel a strong sense of meaning in their lives are more engaged in civic life, volunteering, and helping others. The recent Blue Zones documentary captured what many people have discovered–that purpose can make us healthier and more resilient as we age.[44] It can

---

[41] Sinek, S. (2009). *Start with why: How great leaders inspire everyone to take action*. Penguin.

[42] Frankl, V. E. (1985). *Man's search for meaning*. Simon and Schuster.

[43] Pattakos, A., & Dundon, E. (2014). *The OPA! way: Finding joy & meaning in everyday life & work*. BenBella Books, Inc.

[44] https://www.bluezones.com/documentary/

help us avoid burnout or despair, and it connects us to other human beings.[45]

Purpose is not the same as a goal. Purpose is a long-term, guiding force in life while goals are specific shorter-term wins linked to actions that help us live out our purpose. Whereas our goals can (and often should) change, purpose is more enduring. Your purpose might be to help others lift themselves up during challenging times. Or, your purpose might be guiding others to gain physical strength and resilience or connect with spiritual faith. There are many examples of people who famously live their purpose through their actions over the course of a lifetime. We might wisely adjust our goals in response to changing circumstances, but without losing sight of our larger purpose.

Especially in an age of information overload, we are likely to benefit from gaining clarity on our purpose and using that purpose to guide our social, professional, and political actions. Clarity of purpose helps us decide who we'll follow–and who we won't. It helps us determine which information is essential and which we might ignore. Purpose also motivates us to act in ways that contribute to powerful collective impact.

---

[45] Buettner, D., & Skemp, S. (2016). Blue zones: Lessons from the world's longest lived. *American Journal of Lifestyle Medicine, 10*(5), 318-321.

Practice 4: Choose Action Over Cynicism

"You can't be neutral on a moving train" - Howard Zinn

Although it's easy to feel like existing systems and actors make change impossible, we urge all of us to step into our own agency and reject stories that strip us of our power. Paulo Freire, who wrote about oppression and education, argued that we must understand the forces that limit us–poverty, discrimination, unjust systems–without denying our ability to act against suffering and injustice.[46] Viktor Frankl argued that, even when we cannot control our circumstances, we can choose how we respond.[47] These individuals aren't ignoring terrible suffering or injustice; they are urging us to resist feeling powerless or cynical. Personal actions such as speaking out, learning, or coming to the defense of others require us to step into power–even if our stride is short at first.

Polarizing mental frames can also keep us trapped in a space where it's hard to create or generate support for social action. When we see most issues as simple opposites—good vs. bad, us vs. them, right vs. wrong—we can get stuck in a cycle where no real progress happens. This kind of thinking, known as *polarity thinking*, makes it hard to find creative solutions or work together. Instead of seeing complex challenges as problems to be "solved" once and for all, Polarity Management teaches that many issues involve interdependent values in tension—like freedom and security,

---

[46] Freire, P. (1967/1996). *Pedagogy of the oppressed*. Continuum.
[47] Frankl, V. E. (1985). *Man's search for meaning*. Simon and Schuster.

tradition and innovation, or individual rights and community responsibility.[48] If we focus only on one side and ignore the other, we are more likely to contribute to resistance, division, and gridlock. Long-term success often comes from managing, not eliminating, these tensions by shifting from an either-or to both-and thinking.

Our ability to engage critically and even skeptically is crucial to navigating our information age. But sliding into cynicism threatens our ability to form healthy relationships and cooperate to take action and solve problems. Cynicism assumes corruption and failure are inevitable and Stanford psychologist Jamil Zaki warns us that "cynicism makes it harder to metabolize the calories of social life to receive nourishment from the people around us."[49] We sometimes engage in cynicism to protect ourselves from uncertainty or disappointment, but a cynical mindset actually contributes to poorer health and reduced impact. Steven Maier and Martin Seligman's research on learned helplessness also shows how we're likely to stop trying to create change when we believe our actions don't matter.[50] Jamil Zaki suggests leaning into *hopeful skepticism* as an alternative to cynicism. Hope is not blind optimism–it is the idea that things could get better–and skepticism pushes us to stay curious like scientists. As skeptics, we don't fall into a single polarity by assuming people are always self-serving or

---

[48] Johnson, B. (1993). Polarity management. *Executive Development, 6*, 28-28.
[49] Zaki, J. (2025, January 15). *Cynicism is a trap. Here's why 'hopeful skepticism' is better* (T. Gross, Interviewer) [Interview transcript]. NPR. https://www.npr.org/transcripts/g-s1177-41448
[50] Maier, S. F., & Seligman, M. E. (2016). Learned helplessness at fifty: Insights from neuroscience. *Psychological review, 123*(4), 349-367. https://doi.org/10.1037/rev0000033

always altruistic. Instead, we wait for evidence in our own lives to determine who we can trust and believe in. We ask tough questions, think critically, and keep pushing for solutions.

What it looks like in action:

Some prominent leaders and activists have shown us how embracing agency–even in dangerous situations–can contribute to powerful social change. For example, Malala Yousafzai was denied education under Taliban rule in Pakistan but, instead of accepting her position within an unjust system, she spoke out, survived an assassination attempt, and became a global symbol of resistance and an advocate for girls' education.[51] American lawyer Bryan Stevenson, founder of the Equal Justice initiative, fights against racial injustice in our U.S. legal system.[52] He speaks powerfully about the deep systemic barriers that continue to contribute to injustice while still doing the daily work to influence laws, help free innocent prisoners, and educate the public about injustice.

Of course, many of us take agency in smaller but collectively meaningful ways. Communities impacted by natural disasters rebuild together and become more resilient rather than waiting for outside help. Grassroots movements empower individuals to take small actions together in the face of major crises and injustices. We might speak out at a public meeting, call our political representatives, or organize a food drive for our local homeless shelter. When we find ways to nurture our sense of agency, we are in a better position to center ourselves, support others, and take a stand aligned with our purpose.

---

[51] https://malala.org/malalas-story
[52] https://justmercy.eji.org/

Community leaders like Kai Degner of Harrisonburg, Virginia are experimenting with *polarity management* to help community members navigate common organizing tensions such as the belief that change starts locally versus the belief that national organizations should be responsible for leading change.[53] Kai urges groups to identify and consciously pursue ways of balancing organizing tensions that get us beyond polarizing beliefs. For example, a balanced approach might seek to anchor activism in local efforts while coordinating with national organizations to gain resources and amplify messaging.

Moving from cynicism to action may also involve adopting new frameworks or tools to move around obstacles–for example, scholars are offering alternatives to current Diversity, Equity, and Inclusion (DEI) strategy. Lily Zheng offers a FAIR Framework as an evidence-based approach for building more just and equitable organizations in a way that aligns with a broad set of American values.[54] Researcher Siri Chilazi suggests embedding this type of fairness strategy into our everyday practices at every level of an organization rather than relying on special programs or periodic training to create change.[55]

---

[53] Johnson, B. (1993). Polarity management. *Executive Development, 6*, 28-28.
[54] https://hbr.org/2025/01/what-comes-after-dei
[55] https://sirichilazi.com/

Actions you can take:

On Your Own:

- Pick one small social or political action to take each day or each week. For example, the 5 Calls website offers you an easy way to contact your political representatives.[56]
- Identify and sideline activities that sap your sense of agency (e.g., stop doom-scrolling, shift news and social media apps off your homescreen, etc.).
- Identify and celebrate everyday people and organizations defying the odds to have meaningful influence in your community and beyond.
- Identify an organization working on an issue you care about and commit to supporting it.
- Send a thank you message to a political or organizational leader who has acted to address a problem impacting your community. Ask them how you can support their work!

With Others:

- Map your collaborators–even if it starts with just one other person, identify people you can work with to make a difference on an issue that matters to you. Don't worry about impact at first–just start identifying your allies.
- Join or form a group or association in your community or region that is committed to taking action on social or political issues–begin with small, concrete actions to build confidence.

---

[56] https://5calls.org

- Share a constructive change example with your organization or network each week.

- Spend at least as much time plotting actions as you do lamenting current circumstances–even when your impact is minimal, you're likely to improve your own outlook and health!

- Adopt new frameworks or tools to move around obstacles–scan for ideas from organizers, academics, and people within your community.

- Identify mental polarities that may be keeping you and your collaborators from moving towards action and seek a productive way to balance these tensions.

- Attend online or in-person meetings with legislators and share hard-hitting questions.

Practice 5: Let Your 'Why' Drive Your Actions

"The purpose of life is not to be happy. It is to be useful, to be honorable, to be compassionate, to have it make some difference that you have lived and lived well."

– Ralph Waldo Emerson

"Many people have a wrong idea of what constitutes true happiness. It is not attained through self-gratification, but through fidelity to a worthy purpose."

– Helen Keller

Many people describe being paralyzed by the speed of social change and chaos in our political arena. Research on both social activism and burnout suggest we can make our efforts more impactful and sustainable by tapping into our deeper sense of purpose–our 'why'–to prioritize and guide our actions. Shawn Ginwright, in his work on healing-centered engagement, urges us not just to resist injustice, but to cultivate joy, hope, and personal fulfillment.[57] When we root our activism in a clear sense of personal mission and vision of the future we aim to create–whether it's building stronger neighborhoods, advancing racial and economic equity, or improving public safety–our effort becomes more than just a reaction to a problem. It becomes a source of meaning we can

---

[57] Ginwright, S. (2018). The future of healing: Shifting from trauma informed care to healing centered engagement. *Occasional Paper, 25*, 25-32.

tap into for inspiration and energy. We are also more likely to work from our strengths and feel less overwhelmed by each emerging crisis when we keep our primary 'why' front and center.

Research by scholars like Marshall Ganz[58], who studies leadership and organizing, shows that we are more likely to follow through on activism when we set specific and achievable goals rather than abstract ideals. For example, instead of saying "I want to fight climate change," a more effective approach would be, "I will start an online group to promote and implement ideas for reducing energy use at home." This makes action more manageable and helps us implement small, consistent actions over time. Research on habits also suggests that we are more likely to stick with commitments when we connect actions to other activities in our daily lives and build in accountability by joining a group or partnering with someone and communicating our commitment publicly.[59][60] Sustainable civic engagement is not just about reacting to emerging crises, but about building a *lifestyle* of meaningful engagement.

What it looks like in action:

Successful social change efforts have long directed people's passions, energy, and talents in concrete and strategic ways. Leaders of the farm workers labor movement, Dolores Huerta and César Chávez, set specific and strategic goals such as organizing

---

[58] Ganz, M., Nohria, N., & Khurana, R. (2010). Leading change. In *Handbook of Leadership Theory and Practice: A Harvard Business School Centennial Colloquium* (pp. 527-568). Harvard Business Review Press.

[59] Duhigg, C. (2012). *The power of habit: Why we do what we do in life and business*. Random House.

[60] Clear, J. (2018). *Atomic habits: Tiny changes, remarkable results*. Avery.

grape boycotts to pressure growers into recognizing unions.[61] They also shared personal stories of workers' suffering to connect with broader audiences in a way that aligns with the practice of *making local suffering tangible*. They built a disciplined and structured movement over time, training and mobilizing thousands of community leaders to engage in strikes, petition drives, and consumer boycotts. They won landmark labor victories because they were able to transform outrage into action.

Women also gained the ability to vote through focused, goal-driven collective action.[62] Early suffragists focused on state-by-state legal battles, but later activities took a more direct and socially engaged approach after progress stalled. They used public protests, hunger strikes, and strategic lobbying to push for a federal amendment. Activists also targeted political leaders directly, staging daily pickets outside the White House–the first time protesters had done this in U.S. history. They issued clear demands and used persuasive messaging that tied their struggle to America's democratic ideals and wartime rhetoric about freedom and justice. This combination of goal-oriented grassroots engagement and persistent and visible action secured women's right to vote nationwide in 1920. More recently, the successful Marriage Equality Movement (2000s-2015) combined clear step-by-step goals, grassroots engagement, and a powerful moral argument

---

[61] https://libraryguides.nau.edu/c.php?g=1306068&p=9598920
[62] https://www.americanbar.org/groups/public_education/programs/19th-amendment-centennial/toolkit/suffrage-timeline/

rooted in human dignity to secure rights for same-sex couples and their families.[63]

Actions you can take:

On Your Own:

- Journal and reflect to clarify a meaningful or pressing 'why' to focus your energy and establish manageable goals. Numerous resources are available to support you in doing this if you are new to this effort. Meredith Walters offers some useful guidance.[64]

- Complete a free online Values Assessment to help you prioritize activities that align with your values.[65]

- Research social action that addresses your 'why'. What has been successful in the past? Who is doing work on this issue now? The University of Washington 'Mapping American Social Movements' website offers excellent information on the activities, membership, and location of various U.S. social movements.[66] You can also use new generative AI tools like ChatGPT to provide initial information on social movements in the news (just take steps to verify this information).[67]

- Set aside a weekly or daily 'action hour' to engage in social action and advance a cause you care about–replace some of the

---

[63] https://www.hrc.org/our-work/stories/the-journey-to-marriage-equality-in-the-united-states
[64] https://meredithwalters.com/clarify-purpose-personal-mission-statement/
[65] https://personalvalu.es/
[66] https://depts.washington.edu/moves/
[67] https://chatgpt.com/

time you spend absorbing news with time you spend helping to make news!

With Others:

- Work with groups that move beyond grievances to articulate concrete goals or demands aligned with your 'why'.

- Organize a discussion group to help participants align their activism with their deeper purpose.

- Prioritize collective action opportunities–look for places where thousands or millions of people taking a small step in their daily lives can add up to something larger.

- Collaborate with friends, family members, neighbors, or colleagues who can help you sustain energy, maintain your focus, and celebrate small wins.

- If you find it hard to narrow your focus when so many issues feel important, take time to differentiate more and less-intensive social actions (i.e., volunteering to lead public forums versus signing petitions or boycotting a single product) and only dedicate time to intensive actions that align with your 'why'.

Practice 6: Consume Mindfully

"The cost of a thing is the amount of...life [that] is required to be exchanged for it, immediately or in the long run."

– Henry David Thoreau

Countless studies, books, and documentaries show us how our culture's excessive emphasis on rapid consumption is harming our communities, our environment, and our own health. Collectively, we are voracious consumers of unhealthy foods, toxic online content, and non-essential consumer products of questionable quality and value. Cycles of purposeless consumption keep many of us anxious, exhausted, and less likely to mobilize for change. Our consumer culture pressures many of us to spend beyond our means to pursue or maintain social status. Some of us work longer or harder than we need to in order to buy fancier clothes or cars or the latest device that quickly becomes obsolete.[68]

In the U.S., success is often measured by wealth, using narrow indicators like stock market performance, GDP, and individual income. Such measures ignore our rapidly growing income inequality, gig economy challenges, automation pressures, and the hidden costs of over-consumption.[69] Many of our most popular streaming shows and influencers flaunt wealth and excess

---

[68] Schor, J. (1998). The overspent american. *Multinational Monitor, 19*(9), p21-24.

[69] Stiglitz, J. E. (2012). *The price of inequality: How today's divided society endangers our future.* WW Norton & Company.

consumption as key to happiness. Online retailers like Amazon use increasingly sophisticated algorithms to influence our buying habits so we purchase more products at higher prices.[70] Yet, most social science research suggests more money does not actually make us happier beyond what it takes to be stable and secure. Psychologist Barry Schwartz, in his book chapter *The Paradox of Choice*, explains how having too many consumer options can actually overwhelm us, leaving us stressed and dissatisfied rather than fulfilled.[71]

Mindless–sometimes obsessive–online activities are also reducing our collective mental health and threatening the well-being of our children.[72] Technology designers leverage psychological insights and data about our habits to keep us clicking and scrolling in ways that rarely support our personal 'why' or our mental and physical health. 24/7 news cycles and social media can overwhelm us, making us feel powerless against misinformation, online harassment, or unhealthy social comparisons.[73] Some political leaders and social influencers actively take advantage of these technology platforms to hijack our focus and keep us feeling disempowered. Algorithms used by media outlets and social media platforms emphasize negative news–like crime, disasters, and political conflicts–to grab our attention. We absorb and repost

---

[70] Van Loo, R., & Aggarwal, N. (2023). Amazon's Pricing Paradox. *Harvard Journal of Law & Technology, 37*(1), 1-56.

[71] Schwartz, B. (2015). The paradox of choice. In *Positive Psychology in Practice: Promoting Human Flourishing in Work, Health, Education, and Everyday Life* (pp. 121-138). John Wiley & Sons.

[72] Haidt, J. (2024). *The anxious generation: How the great rewiring of childhood is causing an epidemic of mental illness.* Random House.

[73] Knight, R. (2025). How to keep up with the news without getting overwhelmed. *Harvard Business Review.*

troubling news and grievances, often without offering or taking meaningful action online or in our communities. Psychologists argue that this constant exposure to negative stories leaves us feeling like the world is more dangerous and hopeless than it really is. While it is important for us to stay generally informed, a more intentional social media and news diet will help us become *hopeful skeptics* rather than paralyzed cynics.

What it looks like in action:

When big decisions or events feel too overwhelming to influence, you can strengthen your sense of agency by taking steps to consume more mindfully in your daily life. You might join a movement to support local businesses, eat healthier foods, or experiment with limits on social media consumption in your household. Many organizations and experts offer advice on shopping and eating more mindfully. For example, The Blue Zone initiative partners with community organizations and businesses to help individuals and communities make better-informed choices about the foods, activities, and beliefs that help us live longer, healthier lives.[74] You might choose to streamline and organize your environment, letting go of things that no longer serve you. Organizational consultant Marie Kondo argues that a deep cleaning to prioritize things that matter (bring us joy!) helps us make better decisions about what to buy in the future.[75] Gretchen Rubin also shows how organizing our environment can leave us feeling calmer and happier.[76] You can make this a win-win effort by donating

---

[74] https://www.bluezones.com

[75] Kondo, M. (2014). *The life-changing magic of tidying up: The Japanese art of decluttering and organizing.* Ten Speed Press.

[76] https://gretchenrubin.com/getting-started-organization/

useful items to support disaster or domestic violence victims to reduce local suffering and support human dignity.

Financial boycotts and Buy Nothing movements coordinate our individual efforts to reduce consumption, aiming us towards a shared purpose. In the 1980s, social activists urged individuals and organizations to stop buying South African products to protest the country's racist apartheid system. Major companies and institutions, including universities and pension funds, divested from South African businesses, cutting off economic support. The resulting financial strain contributed to the eventual dismantling of apartheid. Boycotts of individual products or companies require time and patience as well as coordination across organizations. Longer-term boycotts are more likely to maintain momentum when coordinators help us keep one eye on the larger purpose and the other eye on small wins in our daily lives. For example, in boycotting an agricultural company that harms the environment, we might also switch to eating healthier foods and feel better about our own diet and health.

Cutting back on digital over-consumption can also help us reduce stress and take action. Writer and journalist Johann Hari draws on many studies and examples to show how time in our virtual world fragments our attention and steals time from our immediate relationships and activities in our physical world.[77] Movements like Digital Minimalism, championed by author Cal Newport, invite us to be more intentional with our screen time by focusing on meaningful activities and limiting the time we give to

---

[77] Hari, J. (2023). *Stolen focus: Why you can't pay attention–And how to think deeply again*. Crown.

our technology.[78] Numerous news outlets report a growing U.S. movement to support smartphone-free childhoods or phone-free schools and numerous states and school districts are considering policies to reduce cell phone use in schools.[79]

Actions you can take:

On Your Own:

- Experiment with a time or consumption log for 2-3 weeks to help you determine how your time, energy, or money support your 'why' and your values.

- Challenge yourself to shop primarily in-person rather than online for 30 days (for those worried about added costs: many online retailers like Amazon no longer offer the most competitive deals).

- Thin out your own possessions to prioritize what matters most while donating to disaster relief organizations.

- Pick one new locally owned business to support regularly.

- Challenge yourself to spend one week buying only what is essential.

- Support companies that build their brand around mindful consumption and sustainable business practices (like Imperfect Foods[80] or Patagonia's Worn Wear program[81]).

---

[78] Newport, C. (2019). *Digital minimalism: Choosing a focused life in a noisy world.* Penguin.

[79] https://www.nea.org/nea-today/all-news-articles/take-cellphones-out-classroom-educators-say

[80] https://www.imperfectfoods.com/

[81] https://wornwear.patagonia.com/

- Pre-schedule a block of time for reviewing daily news so negative information doesn't keep tugging on your time and attention throughout the day.
- Remove news apps from your phone and switch to traditional print news sources if you find yourself unable to stop scrolling through online news throughout the day.
- Take an hour or two to unsubscribe from any unnecessary emails or junk/spam messages that add distraction in your inbox.
- Unsubscribe from social media platforms that don't take reasonable steps to moderate content that incites hate, division, and violence. If you aren't yet ready to unsubscribe, but want to send a message and protect your privacy, you can limit how your data is used. To set limits on how Meta/Facebook/Instagram use your data, view the Electronic Frontier Foundation guidance.[82]

With Others:

- Participate in or organize 'Buy Nothing' or boycott movements to take a political stand while modeling more mindful consumption.
- Align your local financial boycotts with boycotts organized by other groups or nations to increase impact.

---

[82] https://www.eff.org/deeplinks/2025/01/mad-meta-dont-let-them-collect-and-monetize-your-personal-data

- Coordinate a mass-request that personal data be removed from a company that is profiting from social division and/or political manipulation.
- Support legislation that increases individual (consumer) control over whether or not to let vendors track buying habits within and across platforms.
- Establish technology-free time in your home and/or local schools.
- Take a technology-free vacation, or "staycation," with family or friends at least once a year.
- Support or participate in youth-driven initiatives to reduce smartphone use by children and teens.

Section Two Action Plan to Support My Purpose

We recommend starting with just one or two actions from this section as you experiment with building or strengthening your civic habits. Add and document your own action ideas as well!

Actions I'll Take	
1.	
With Whom?	**By When?**
2.	
With Whom?	**By When?**
3.	
With Whom?	**By When?**
4.	
With Whom?	**By When?**

Section Two Action Lessons

Consider jotting down lessons learned from any actions you've taken in this section.

1. **What impact I believe I've had with my actions (for myself and for others):**

2. **What, if anything, surprised me:**

3. **What I learned that will help me in the future:**

Section Three: Joy

Throughout history, joy has played a crucial role in motivating us to act and sustain our efforts. Finding joy during troubled times is not the same thing as staying optimistic. Harvard psychologist Susan David warns that excessive optimism or positivity can become toxic when we maintain it relentlessly and suppress our other emotions.[83] The good news is that we can be anxious or skeptical and still tap into joy because joy is an embodied, present-moment experience that often emerges during collective actions, celebrations, or rituals. Joy does not negate or ignore suffering; it simply allows us to find meaning, pleasure, and hope in modest–often unexpected–experiences. Unlike fear or rage, which can lead to burnout, joy helps us be more resilient by reinforcing our sense of purpose and connection. Brené Brown argues that joy is often deeply rooted in gratitude, connection, and meaning.[84]

Neuroscience helps explain why joy is such a powerful motivator. Positive emotions like joy activate our brain's mesolimbic reward system, which increases our dopamine levels and makes us more motivated to act.[85] Studies suggest that we are more likely to stay engaged in hard tasks and persist in pursuing

---

[83] David, S. (2016). *Emotional agility: Get unstuck, embrace change, and thrive in work and life.* Penguin.

[84] Brown, B. (2021). *Atlas of the heart: Mapping meaningful connection and the language of human experience.* Random House.

[85] Davidson, R. J. (2012). *The emotional life of your brain: How its unique patterns affect the way you think, feel, and live--And how you can change them.* Penguin.

our purpose when we experience moments of joy. Social movements, from the Civil Rights Movement in the U.S. to anti-apartheid activism in South Africa, have long relied on collective joy. People turn to music, dance, artistic creation, and celebration as a way to strengthen bonds, sustain motivation, and remind each other of the world they are working to create. Of course, finding joy requires us to engage directly with experiences rather than being a passive observer. Much research and writing also suggests we are more likely to find joy when we act in relationship to other people.

In *The Book of Joy* (2016), co-written by the Dalai Lama and Archbishop Desmond Tutu, two deeply reflective spiritual leaders from different faiths describe how gratitude and helping others can shift our focus away from what we lack and towards what we already have in our lives.[86] This mindset helps us cultivate joy by reducing our focus on fleeting desires and reinforcing a sense of connection and contentment. Emerging neuroscientific research supports this idea, showing that gratitude and giving to others activates our brain regions associated with positive emotions and well-being.[87] All of this suggests that joy—though it may sometimes feel distant in dark times—is an essential ingredient for constructing a more just and humane world.

---

[86] Lama, D., Tutu, D., & Abrams, D. C. (2016). *The book of joy: Lasting happiness in a changing world*. Penguin.

[87] Harbaugh, W. T., Mayr, U., & Burghart, D. R. (2007). Neural responses to taxation and voluntary giving reveal motives for charitable donations. *Science, 316*(5831), 1622-1625.

Practice 7: Move Your Body

"All that is important is this one moment in movement. Make the moment important, vital, and worth living. Do not let it slip away unnoticed and unused."

– Martha Graham

For many of us, a large percentage of our work and/or social life happens online today. This means it's easy for us to ignore our bodies. We pay less attention to our physical sensations and get worse at understanding what our body is trying to tell us. When we disconnect from physical sensations—like hunger, fatigue, pain, or stress—we risk pushing ourselves beyond healthy limits, increasing our risk of burnout or illness.[88] Ignoring physical cues like exhaustion or discomfort can leave us more vulnerable to physical weakness, accidents, or injury. If we want to experience joy, it starts with moving our body, even if that just means breathing more deeply. If we want to make a difference in the world, we need to learn to listen to our bodies again.

Researchers have found that physical movement plays a major role in boosting our motivation and well-being.[89][90] Exercise

---

[88] Puolitaival, T., Sieppi, M., Pyky, R., Enwald, H., Korpelainen, R., & Nurkkala, M. (2020). Health behaviours associated with video gaming in adolescent men: a cross-sectional population-based MOPO study. *BMC Public Health, 20*, 1-8.

[89] Ratey, J. J., & Loehr, J. E. (2011). The positive impact of physical activity on cognition during adulthood: A review of underlying mechanisms, evidence and recommendations. *Reviews in the Neurosciences 22*(2), 171-185.

[90] Hardy, L. L., Ding, D., Peralta, L. R., Mihrshahi, S., & Merom, D. (2018). Association between sitting, screen time, fitness domains, and fundamental

releases endorphins and dopamine–chemicals in the brain that improve mood and energy.[91] We don't have to be super athletes to take advantage of this insight. Studies show that even light movement like walking, stretching, or dancing can reduce stress, increase motivation, and help us be more creative. Research also shows that moving in nature often produces feelings of awe–a sense that arises when we encounter something vast, powerful, or beautiful. Awe is an emotion linked to increased happiness, humility, and social connectedness, and psychologists like Dacher Keltner have found that experiences of awe triggered by movement in nature can boost our creativity and prosocial behavior, making us more motivated to be in community and support others.[92]

Beyond personal well-being, movement is also deeply connected to social action and change. Major social movements and campaigns bring people together in physical presence–whether gathering at a community meeting, moving together in protest, or holding silent space in a vigil.

What it looks like in action:

During the COVID-19 pandemic, movement became both a risk and a necessity for many of us. Public health restrictions limited gatherings and disrupted our rituals of shared movement such as athletic games and religious gatherings. Yet people around the world adapted, finding ways to move through walking, virtual

---

motor skills in children aged 5–16 years: Cross-sectional population study. *Journal of Physical Activity and Health*, *15*(12), 933-940.

[91] Basso, J. C., & Suzuki, W. A. (2016). The effects of acute exercise on mood, cognition, neurophysiology, and neurochemical pathways: A review. *Brain Plasticity*, *2*(2), 127-152.

[92] Keltner, D. (2009). *Born to be good: The science of a meaningful life*. WW Norton & Company.

dance classes, and other forms of socially distanced exercise. Social movements like the volunteer-led Parkrun helped people get outdoors and moving together.[93] Parkrun, a global initiative launched in the UK in 2004, organizes free community-based runs and walks in green spaces around the world each week. The movement emphasizes social connection and physical activity for community well-being, and research shows participation in Parkrun reduces loneliness, improves mental health, and strengthens community ties.

Embodied activity can also be a powerful form of protest. In multiple South American countries, embodied vigils conducted in the name of disappeared relatives have had a significant impact. Across countries like Argentina and Chile, families of the disappeared–often led by women–have used their physical presence to demand justice, truth, and accountability. Activists used embodied demonstrations to keep the memory of loved ones alive while they pressured governments and human rights organizations to act. In the U.S. and around the world, Black Lives Matter brought protesters into the streets to use their bodies to demonstrate the urgency of racial justice efforts following the murder of George Floyd in 2020. In 2011, Occupy Wall Street protesters occupied public spaces in tents in a highly visible and embodied demonstration to highlight income inequality and corporate influence in U.S. politics following the 2008 financial crisis.

---

[93] Wiltshire, G., & Merchant, S. (2021). What can we learn about nature, physical activity, and health from Parkrun?. In *Nature and Health* (pp. 208-222). Routledge.

Actions you can take:

On Your Own:

- Walk, dance, or jog to get your body moving regularly throughout the day–even if it's just 5 or 10 minutes of movement at a time.
- Get outside into nature–whether in a park, forest, or garden–to shift your mindset, reduce stress, or solve problems.
- Use your breath to center and calm yourself by meditating or using tactical breathing techniques often used by athletes, members of the military, and first responders to reduce stress and regain focus.[94]

With Others:

- Ask a friend or coworker to turn online coffee chats or video meetings into walking conversations.
- Participate in collective physical movement via a local group or national organization like Parkrun.[95]
- If you love to dance, look for an Ecstatic Dance or 5 Rhythms class near you to dance out your emotions and generate new ideas.[96][97]

---

[94] https://www.med.navy.mil/Portals/62/Documents/NMFA/NMCPHC/root/Documents/health-promotion-wellness/psychological-emotional-wellbeing/Combat-Tactical-Breathing.pdf
[95] https://www.parkrun.us
[96] https://ecstaticdance.org/
[97] https://www.5rhythms.com/

- Attend a public meeting in-person, using your body to show solidarity.
- Engage in creative, embodied protests.
- Join or organize others to use creative expression–painting, dancing, etc.–to convey important social or political messages in an embodied way.
- Play a game of tag or hide-and-seek with kids to add some joyful movement to your day.

Practice 8: Gather

"There is no power for change greater than a community discovering what it cares about."

– Margaret J. Wheatley

In 2023, the U.S. Surgeon General issued a report on the "Epidemic of Loneliness and Isolation," warning us that social isolation is having disastrous effects on our mental and physical health.[98] Approximately half of America's adult population has reported experiencing loneliness in recent years, and research identifies loneliness as a key factor in numerous negative health outcomes. Factors such as remote work, social media, and pandemic-era distancing have reduced our face-to-face interactions in recent years. Researchers have also pointed to busy lifestyles, economic pressures, a car-based culture, and the loss of community spaces like local clubs, religious groups, and neighborhood gatherings.[99] Overall, this loneliness makes us less resilient, less trusting, and more susceptible to manipulation by divisive leaders.

---

[98] Office of the Surgeon General. (2023). *Our epidemic of loneliness and isolation: The U.S. Surgeon General's advisory on the healing effects of social connection and community*. U.S. Department of Health and Human Services. https://www.hhs.gov/sites/default/files/surgeon-general-social-connection-advisory.pdf

[99] Putnam, R. D. (2000). *Bowling alone: The collapse and revival of American community*. Simon and Schuster.

Political theorist Hannah Arendt viewed loneliness as much more than a personal issue.[100] Arendt fled Nazi Germany in 1933, and her experiences during the rise of Nazism deeply shaped her thinking and quest to understand the conditions that lead to totalitarianism. According to Arendt, authoritarian leaders can use our loneliness to their advantage, offering a sense of identity, purpose, and belonging even if it is based on extremist ideology and hostility towards other groups. She warned that societies experiencing widespread loneliness are especially vulnerable to manipulation and the rise of authoritarian rule by leaders who promise a strong sense of purpose and connection. Arendt's work suggests that building meaningful social connections is not a luxury, but a crucial ingredient for democratic societies.

Real human relationships anchor us in a chaotic and uncertain world. When we face great threats–whether political or environmental–authentic social connections can support us emotionally, socially, and politically. The simple act of sitting together, sharing food, and trading stories can bring us joy and help us push back against isolation, fear, and hopelessness. Shared laughter releases endorphins—the brain's natural "feel-good" chemicals—reducing stress, improving our mood, and even temporarily relieving our pain.[101][102] Psychologist Gillian

---

[100] Arendt, H. (1951/1973). *The origins of totalitarianism*. Harcourt, Brace, Jovanovich.

[101] Mayo Clinic (2023). Stress relief from laughter: It's no joke. https://www.mayoclinic.org/healthy-lifestyle/stress-management/in-depth/stress-relief/art-20044456

[102] Zhao, J., Yin, H., Zhang, G., Li, G., Shang, B., Wang, C., & Chen, L. (2019). A meta-analysis of randomized controlled trials of laughter and humour interventions on depression, anxiety and sleep quality in adults. *Journal of Advanced Nursing*, 75(11), 2435-2448.

Sandstrom's studies show that even brief conversations we have with strangers, neighbors, or people we regularly encounter while running errands make us feel happier and more connected.[103]

Although it may be tempting to reduce social interactions and contact with people who do not share our social or political views, this is likely to fuel the dangerous dynamics Arendt describes. Of course, we also benefit from feeling safe and connected in communities that share our worldviews and concerns, so this is a polarity we'll need to navigate intentionally. We might, for example, seek to gather more frequently beginning with close friends and family and then extend our efforts to engage in semi-structured gatherings with people who hold notably different worldviews and perspectives. Here, Peter Coleman's research on conflict may be helpful. He offers a number of insights, including the finding that physically moving in sync with someone–like walking together–can actually prompt neurological tendencies in us that increase our compassion and empathy for that person even if we disagree with them.[104]

What it looks like in action:

Connectors–individuals who naturally build large networks of friends and acquaintances–often initiate gatherings and bring others together by making introductions and bridging different social circles. Malcolm Gladwell argues that their influence isn't just about knowing many people, but it's their genuine interest in

---

[103] Sandstrom, G. M., & Dunn, E. W. (2014). Social interactions and well-being: The surprising power of weak ties. *Personality and Social Psychology Bulletin, 40*(7), 910-922.

[104] Coleman, P. (2022, February 8). To resolve conflicts, get up and move. *Greater Good Magazine: Science-Based Insights for a Meaningful Life.*

human relationships that gives connectors the ability to make so many meaningful introductions.[105] On a smaller scale, community connectors exist in almost every neighborhood or town: the local librarian who organizes community events, the neighbor who introduces other neighbors to each other, or the volunteer who regularly gathers people for local causes.

A number of organizations also use social media tools to help volunteers gather and collaborate to strengthen community services and relationships. Organizations like MeetUp leverage social media tools to help people make connections more easily and come together around shared interests, hobbies, and passions.[106] CommunityShare connects K-12 educators with community volunteers in cities around the country to create real-world projects driven by students' passions.[107]

Humans also gather to support each other during and after disasters. Volunteers organize rescue parties, neighbors set up community kitchens, and strangers pull together to offer various forms of relief. For example, communities in California and across the country organized quickly through social media to provide relief for victims of the state's recent wildfires. Neighbors offered their homes as temporary shelters, shared critical information about evacuations, and provided food, clothing, and emotional support to displaced families. Amanda Ripley, who studies the way we respond to disasters, argues that knowing your neighbor

---

[105] Gladwell, M. (2006). *The tipping point: How little things can make a big difference*. Little, Brown.
[106] https://www.meetup.com/
[107] https://www.communityshare.org/

typically matters more than hoarding supplies when it comes to surviving a crisis.[108]

Actions you can take:

On Your Own:

- List your favorite group activities (from recent or past life experience) and identify one or two of these activities to host or organize in the next month.
- Reflect on the possibility that a friend, neighbor, or co-worker with increasingly extreme political views might be suffering from our loneliness epidemic.

With Others:

- Invite a group of friends over for dinner and a movie.
- Pick something you often do alone and invite a friend.
- Stop to talk with a neighbor or stranger you've never met about their baby/child/dog/home.
- Help organize a community activity (e.g., a food drive, trash pick-up, barbecue, etc.) and invite people you wouldn't normally interact with.
- Organize a Parkrun with a diverse group of people in your neighborhood/community or workplace.[109]

---

[108] Ripley, A. (2024). *The unthinkable (revised and updated): Who survives when disaster strikes--And why*. Harmony.

[109] https://www.parkrun.us

- Attend at least one public event, community meeting, church service, or other social activity you would not normally attend each month.
- Organize a group of friends to take political action together (e.g., speaking at a local board meeting, writing your legislators, supporting an emerging political leader).
- Invite someone you disagree with on many things to take a walk or hike with you.
- Invite a friend or neighbor who holds a different political view to join your local Braver Angels chapter with you.[110]
- Join CommunityShare to collaborate with educators and co-create real-world projects for students.[111]

---

[110] https://braverangels.org/
[111] https://www.communityshare.org/

Practice 9: Take the Risks that Matter

"A man dies when he refuses to stand up for that which is right. A man dies when he refuses to stand up for justice. A man dies when he refuses to take a stand for that which is true."

– Martin Luther King, Jr.

"There can be no vulnerability without risk. There can be no community without vulnerability. There can be no peace, and ultimately no life, without community."

– M. Scott Peck

Many of us are on overload–absorbing rapidly evolving news on human conflict, natural disasters, and social ills that feel too big to influence. Even if we care deeply and have a sense for the '*why*' that motivates us most, it's easy to become paralyzed as we survey the chaotic actions of powerful actors or the ecological risks that seem to grow exponentially each time we scan the news. This is where some advice from the east may be useful.

Wu wei (pronounced "woo way") is an ancient Chinese concept that translates roughly to "effortless action."[112] It is not about literally doing nothing, but about moving more naturally with

---

[112] Kee, Y. H., Li, C., Zhang, C. Q., & Wang, J. C. K. (2021). The wu-wei alternative: Effortless action and non-striving in the context of mindfulness practice and performance in sport. *Asian Journal of Sport and Exercise Psychology, 1*(2-3), 122-132.

situations instead of forcing things. We might think of it like taking some time to float downstream instead of against the current—harnessing the natural flow of life rather than exhausting ourselves by always struggling against it. During conflict this might mean listening longer before acting, choosing when to speak or act strategically, or redirecting energy rather than getting sucked into someone else's effort to frame an argument or debate. Wu wei discourages a focus on winning any specific argument but suggests that larger battles may still be won by those who make the wisest decisions about when and how to act and when not to act.

We might slow down long enough to ask ourselves questions about how, when, and where to direct our energy. Perhaps making repeated calls to a specific legislator who is up for re-election makes more sense than posting a bunch of messages to various social media sites. Maybe joining a human rights campaign organized by your faith community feels more energizing than writing emails or letters to your political representatives on your own. If your voice doesn't feel loud enough, you might amplify your influence by urging a local community organizer, political leader, faith leader, or online influencer to speak up. A Wu wei orientation does not mean inaction; it means we will be prepared to act with greater clarity, strategy, and resolve when the time is right. Although it may seem counterintuitive, even stillness and rest represent a form of action, helping us stay centered and clear-headed. Much has been written recently about the way different forms of rest help us recharge, fight burnout, and improve our mental health.[113] When we are

---

[113] Hammond, C. (2019). *The art of rest: How to find respite in the modern age*. Canongate Books.

sufficiently rested, we will be better at channeling our energy and skills to act where it matters.

What it looks like in action:

Throughout history, people have taken both extraordinary and everyday risks to support a healthier and more just society. Some have put their lives or jobs on the line—civil rights activists facing violent backlash during desegregation or whistleblowers exposing corruption despite the risk to their jobs or professional status. During the U.S. civil rights movement, Freedom Riders, including both Black and white activists, rode buses into the South to challenge segregated transportation. Their willingness to risk beatings, firebombings, and imprisonment exposed the federal government's failure to enforce desegregation laws, and ultimately helped bring an end to segregated transit.

Others take quieter but still meaningful risks. For example, employees challenge unethical workplace policies, citizens speak out in potentially hostile political forums, or neighbors report domestic violence even though they fear retaliation. Even modest acts, like boycotting exploitative companies, refusing to spread misinformation, or standing up to a bully, require courage. These actions—whether dramatic or subtle—are essential to building a world that is more just and compassionate. By taking purposeful action to support human dignity, we also open up more opportunities for joy. Susan McCulley offers three questions to help us stay grounded and take the risks that matter.[114]

1. What is good, beautiful, and working?

---

[114] https://www.susanmcculley.com/blog-posts/waves-3-quesitons

2. Who or what are you willing to stand up for, clasp hands with, and work for?
3. What is your superpower? What do you do well and with joy?

Actions you can take:

On Your Own:

- Sharpen your 'why' to help you determine what you will risk and how you will engage to support human dignity.
- Identify collaborators who are willing to take risks with you.
- Use Susan McCulley's questions and the action plan templates in this guide to help you prioritize where you will put your time and energy.
- Identify a specific fear holding you back from action and challenge yourself to step into it.
- Speak up about any unethical or illegal behavior as a whistleblower in your professional or political role.
- Determine when/if civil disobedience is a necessary action despite the risks and consequences.
- Consider running for political office in your community/region.
- Give and donate what you can for what matters most to you.
- Build periods of rest into your week (e.g,. naps, reflective writing, quiet walks, or meditation).

With Others:

- Publicly celebrate and thank leaders who support human dignity and/or reduce human suffering.

- Share information about *consequential* social and political decisions or events with your network.
- Join or organize a public action (protest, vigil, boycott, art exhibit, etc.) that aligns with your 'why'.
- Join or organize litigation against government agencies, corporations, and leaders engaged in unconstitutional actions.
- Help build alternative governing models that function at the local level when/if government programs become unavailable or insufficient.
- Join boycotts, organized product return movements, or work stoppages when companies threaten democracy or human dignity.
- Participate in campaigning for emerging political leaders who demonstrate a commitment to democracy and human dignity.

Section Three Action Plan to Support Joy

We recommend starting with just one or two actions from this section as you experiment with building or strengthening your civic habits. Add and document your own action ideas as well!

Actions I'll Take	
1.	
With Whom?	**By When?**
2.	
With Whom?	**By When?**
3.	
With Whom?	**By When?**
4.	
With Whom?	**By When?**

Section Three Action Lessons

Consider jotting down lessons learned from any actions you've taken in this section.

1. **What impact I believe I've had with my actions (for myself and for others):**

2. **What, if anything, surprised me:**

3. **What I learned that will help me in the future:**

Onwards!

Thank yourself for investing time and energy to help build a more connected, resilient, and humane nation! We have much to accomplish, but we believe our commitment to acting *together* over time is more crucial than the heroic action of any single leader or special interest group. Throughout our history in the U.S. we have found ways to leverage our diversity of experiences, cultures, and viewpoints to overcome threats to human dignity and continue building a more just society. Setbacks are to be expected, change is inevitable–and the future is still ours to shape. We hope you've discovered some ideas and actions you will share and implement in your community.

Also, please share your actions and ideas with others and access new action resources and practical federal policy updates for our expanding movement at: https://www.OutrageIntoAction.org/

About the Author

S. E. McClellan is a teacher, coach, and consultant who works with individuals and organizations to navigate unprecedented levels of change and uncertainty with curiosity, courage, and mental and emotional agility. McClellan emphasizes exploration and action in support of the public good across sectors and professions and believes we need a whole society response to address wicked problems such as climate change, political polarization, and mental health crises. McClellan's own experiences and research suggest we are all effected to varying degrees by the quality of our social and environmental contexts-and we all have something to offer as well as some responsibility when it comes to improving these contexts.

www.ingramcontent.com/pod-product-compliance
Lightning Source LLC
Chambersburg PA
CBHW020558030426
42337CB00013B/1138